BOOTSTRAPS:

A Step-by-Step Guide from Debt to Financial Independence

MICHAEL A. FLEMING

Copyright © 2018 Michael A. Fleming

All rights reserved.

ISBN: 1-7325565-0-4

ISBN-13: 978-1-7325565-0-8

DEDICATION

This book is dedicated to my parents who instilled in me the value of hard work and education at an early age. Without their rearing, love, and support, I would not be where I am today.

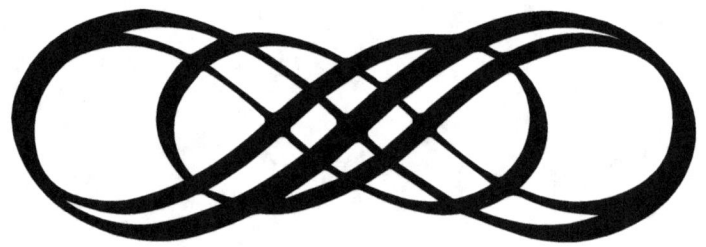

CONTENTS

Dedication iii

Acknowledgments vi

Introduction: About This Book vii

1. From No Money to Financial Independence 1

2. From Debt and Unemployment to
   Investments and Wealth 13

3. Lifestyle Considerations 33

4. Income for Life through Intellectual Property 41

5. Additional Tools to Consider 50

Conclusion 53

About The Author 54

ACKNOWLEDGMENTS

First and foremost, I would like to thank and acknowledge my mom and dad for raising me to be self-reliant and independent. Second, I would like to thank my wife for having patience with me during the writing of this book and for being its first reader. Last but not least, I would like to thank my two brothers for being a constant source of motivation and encouragement.

Introduction: About This Book

This book is guaranteed to improve your financial life and to increase your net worth. The advice given in this book is based on years of personal experience and on the body of knowledge and financial wisdom I have accumulated over the years. This book is intended for anyone who wishes to follow simple but empowering steps to control their financial situation and become financially independent. This book is not intended for those who are seeking business advice but may nonetheless benefit immensely from the steps and advice given. This book is entitled <u>Bootstraps: A Step-by-Step Guide from Debt to Financial Independence</u> and to that end, it is written as a "hand up" to those who wish to improve their lot in life by their own sheer will. With that in mind, let's begin.

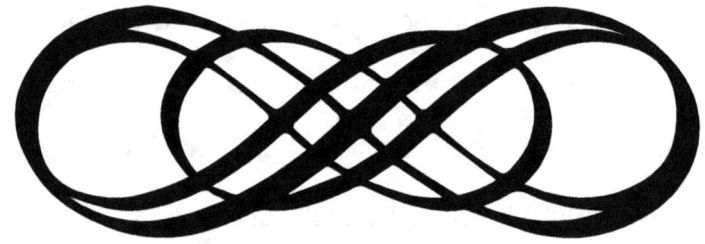

1

FROM NO MONEY TO FINANCIAL INDEPENDENCE

An understanding of personal finance is essential to accumulating and maintaining personal wealth. Personal finance is akin to personal management of one's assets and liabilities. Without this basic understanding, one may find the path to financial independence to be unattainable, not maintainable, or short-lived. Before one can practice personal finance, however, one must first have some money to manage. Therein lies the rub. How does one become wealthy when they have little or no money? In this chapter, we will discuss the main pathways to financial success and how one can achieve financial independence through one or a combination of these pathways.

There are four main pathways to financial success. The first pathway is via **gainful employment**. The second pathway is via **entrepreneurship**. The third pathway is via **investments** and the fourth pathway is via an **intellectual property**. There is a good chance that you may already know someone who has followed each one of these pathways to great financial success. Which pathway or pathways should you take? Before answering this question, let's look into each pathway and get a feel for what each path would entail for financial success.

PATHWAY NO. 1 – GAINFUL EMPLOYMENT

As a group, physicians and surgeons, top executives, and lawyers are among the highest paid employees in the United States.[1,2,3] In 2017, the average physician salary ranged from $187,540 for pediatricians to $265,990 for anesthesiologists.[4] The average chief executive officer

---

1 Bureau of Labor Statistics, U.S. Department of Labor, *Occupational Outlook Handbook*, Physicians and Surgeons, *available at* https://www.bls.gov/ooh/healthcare/physicians-and-surgeons.htm (*last modified June 11, 2018*).
2 Bureau of Labor Statistics, U.S. Department of Labor, *Occupational Outlook Handbook*, Top Executives, *available at* https://www.bls.gov/ooh/management/top-executives.htm (*last modified April 13, 2018*).
3 Bureau of Labor Statistics, U.S. Department of Labor, *Occupational Outlook Handbook*, Lawyers, *available at* https://www.bls.gov/ooh/legal/lawyers.htm (*last modified April 13, 2018*).
4 Bureau of Labor Statistics, U.S. Department of Labor, *Occupational Outlook Handbook*, Physicians and Surgeons, *available at* https://www.bls.gov/ooh/healthcare/physicians-and-surgeons.htm (*last*

(CEO) salary was $107,130 for government sector to $208,000 or more for professional, scientific, and technical services.[5] The average lawyer salary ranged from $85,260 for state government attorneys to $141,900 for attorneys employed by the federal government.[6] These salaries are considerably high considering that the average salary in the United States in 2017 was $50,620.[7]

Do these statistics mean that everyone should become a doctor or a lawyer or a CEO to be financially independent? Not at all. Nonetheless, if you are currently making $50,620 or more a year, you are in the top 50th percentile of wage earners in the United States and have a considerable advantage over your less wealthy counterparts if you manage your money wisely. But what if you make less than $50,620 a year? Is there still a pathway to financial independence? The answer is a resounding *"yes"* and I will show you why.

In terms of pathways, most Americans find themselves employed in order to support themselves and their families. Regardless of your

---

modified June 11, 2018).
5 Bureau of Labor Statistics, U.S. Department of Labor, *Occupational Outlook Handbook*, Top Executives, *available at* https://www.bls.gov/ooh/management/top-executives.htm (*last modified April 13, 2018*).
6 Bureau of Labor Statistics, U.S. Department of Labor, *Occupational Outlook Handbook*, Lawyers, *available at* https://www.bls.gov/ooh/legal/lawyers.htm (*last modified April 13, 2018*).
7 Bureau of Labor Statistics, U.S. Department of Labor, *Occupational Outlook Handbook*, May 2017 National Occupational Employment and Wages Estimates, available at https://www.bls.gov/oes/current/oes_nat.htm#00-0000 (*last modified March 30, 2018*).

level of income, personal finance is key to accumulating wealth. To have wealth to manage, however, you need either:

1) a wealthy relative to give you some money, or

2) a vocation.

While there are those who have wealthy relatives, this book is not a Cinderella story about making money by doing nothing. This book is not even about making money by using other people's money. ***This book is a guide to making wealth by one's own efforts.***

Cinderella is a harmful myth and has created a mindset of marrying rich or playing the lottery in order to get ahead in life. The reality is that the vast majority of Americans do not have a wealthy relative who is willing to finance their path to financial independence. Another reality is that Prince Charming is not real and he (or she) will never come. If you want financial independence, you must work for it. Playing the lottery is not an investment strategy. In fact, if you are playing the lottery, I would adjure you to stop *immediately*. If you have enough money to buy lottery tickets, you have enough money to save and invest. That being said, by understanding personal finance, you will learn to appreciate the value of money and will be able to save more money, i.e., have more money and be financially independent.

Now that we have established the fact that you will have to work in some capacity in order to become financially independent, let's talk about employment. There are two types of jobs in America. There are those jobs which pay well and there are those jobs which do not pay well. Regardless of what type of job(s) you may have, it is incumbent upon you to work and to save money. The better your job pays, the easier it will be to achieve financial independence via the gainful employment pathway. The key to this pathway, however, is **gainful** employment. If you are currently working at a low paying job, your first priority should be to find a way to earn more money. Keep in mind that this may entail finding a better job. Being underemployed is not a crime but it is a waste of labor in the sense that one's personal potential is not being achieved and the society does not benefit as much. For example, a person with a medical degree is more likely to realize his or her full potential as a practicing physician than as a fast food worker. Not only would this person benefit society to a greater extent, this person would also be in a better position to benefit himself or herself financially.

But what if you *are* the fast food worker and you are looking to "pull yourself up by the bootstraps" and become financially independent? There are many options to consider but initially, there are only two – either staying or leaving. If you choose to stay, you should focus your energies on maximizing your potential in terms of what the fast food industry has to offer, namely supervisory and management positions and even opportunities for owning a franchise. One may consider improving their communication and interpersonal skills in order to move up the ladder within the workplace. One may even consider taking business courses in accounting or management which every business needs in order to be successful. By improving your skill set, you are increasing your value to the organization and are more likely than not to improve your financial outlook as well.

But what if you decide that the fast food industry is not for you? Well, before you leave, you should ask yourself the following questions:

1) Do I have another solid job offer to accept? If not, ***don't leave***. It is easier to find a better job when you already have a job. It is harder to find a job when you are unemployed. In fact, you may even do more harm than good to your financial situation if you quit your job and have no job to turn to. Ideally speaking, you should replace your current job with a better job or at least an equivalently paying job which allows for personal growth and development.

2) Am I in a position to return to school to further my education or to get certified in a trade or profession in order to increase my market value? If not, **don't leave**. In the twenty-first century, educational training, either college or vocational, are increasingly more important to being gainfully employed in today's workforce.

As a general rule, one should be working in order to have an income to save and invest. An exception to this rule, however, would be forgoing work for personal development by pursuing education or certification in a given field. Generally speaking, those with advanced degrees and education earn more than those with only a high school diploma and no vocational training. If you haven't already, it would behoove you to consider your strengthens and weaknesses and consider pursuing higher education, training, or certification in a field which piques your interests, provides room for personal growth and development, and compensates you well for your work. Not only will advancing your education be personally rewarding and gratifying, it will also put you on the fast track to being gainfully employed and financially independent.

Pathway No. 2 – Entrepreneurship

Do you have a product or service that you can provide? Do you have enough capital to support your business through market lows? Do you have business acumen and acuity? Of the four main pathways, entrepreneurship may be the most challenging of ways to achieve financial independence. While this pathway is filled with financial risks and uncertainties to overcome, it may also be one of the most rewarding. This pathway, however, is not without some points to consider.

Unlike the gainful employment pathway, entrepreneurship does not provide the comfort or security of a consistent paycheck on a periodic basis. Income will depend not only on personal effort but on market supply and demand. You may have the best ideas about a product or service but ideas are simply not enough. You will need to market your product or service and provide excellent customer service time and time again. You may have to work many unpaid hours for more than 40 hours a week to set up your business and to keep your business running smoothly and without a hitch. Despite all of your best efforts, however, hitches will occur and you will have to minimize them yourself or hire qualified help to handle them. In addition to the responsibility of managing and paying employees, there are also liabilities with profound legal consequences and ramifications to consider. Depending on your business, you may also have considerable overhead to keep your business afloat. On top of all that, there is no guarantee of success and the prospect of failure can be overwhelming. Indeed, starting and running a business can be quite involved and is not for the faint of heart.

Nonetheless, business ownership can be quite rewarding. For many, entrepreneurship is like a calling. Some people just simply have the drive, desire, and motivation to do what it takes to make a business succeed. When done successfully, you are getting paid and having an influence on society. You are at the helm of the ship and you are in control of the direction and future of your business and your employees. You create your own schedule and work as little or as much as necessary to keep your business running smoothly. You are creating jobs and improving the quality of life for many. Not only are you providing a product or service, you are also leaving a legacy for your heirs. The sky is the limit as far as your earning potential is concerned and the prestige of ownership is priceless.

At this point, you may be asking yourself if entrepreneurship is right for you. Because of the highly personal nature of running a business and the challenges that come with it, there is no way I can answer that question for you. The pathway of gainful employment provides a safety net and a sense of security in knowing that you have a paycheck on a consistent basis for time worked. While your earning potential via the gainful employment pathway may be relatively limited, it may be crucial to have that sense of security for yourself and for your family. The pathway of entrepreneurship, however, has the potential to be far more lucrative but is not without risks. Like with the pathway of gainful employment, personal development would be advisable to maximize one's skill set as they pertain to being a successful entrepreneur.

Pathway No. 3 – Investments

The saying that "it takes money to make money" could not be truer for any other pathway than for the investments pathway. The key to financial independence via this pathway is to invest ***often*** and to invest ***consistently***. The concept is simple. To be financially independent, you need to earn more money than you spend. The difference between what you earn and what you spend is your "savings". While your savings may be modest, they can grow substantially over time if you invest them wisely. Before you know it, you will have a nest egg upon which you can choose to retire early or to live out your dreams.

There are many investment vehicles to consider. One may choose to invest in stocks, bonds, mutual funds, ETFs, derivatives, futures, commodities, or precious metals. One may also choose to invest in real estate as well. While there are many pros and cons to each investment type, the underlying investment principle is the same – to make *your money* work for you so that *you* don't have to. Later in this book, I will provide step-by-step advice on how to save money and invest it for maximum returns.

Hopefully, you can see by now that there is a direct relationship between the gainful employment pathway and the investment pathway. Regardless of your financial situation or occupation, you can "pull yourself up by your bootstraps" and achieve financial independence by combining and focusing on these two pathways alone. This book will provide you with step-by-step advice on how to invest your money wisely and on how to apply principles of personal finance to achieve financial independence.

Pathway No. 4 – Intellectual property

The fourth and final pathway to financial independence is by way of intellectual property. The intellectual property pathway entails using creativity and ingenuity to create works of art and inventions which may be marketed or sold with an exclusive right to ownership of concept. Copyrights, patents, and trademarks are all examples of intellectual property. Like the entrepreneurship pathway, the intellectual property pathway has the potential to yield unlimited revenue streams for the talented musician, songwriter, author, computer programmer, or inventor. Unlike the entrepreneurship pathway, however, the initial startup costs may be considerably less for intellectual property.

Should you consider the intellectual property pathway as a means to financial independence? Most definitely! If you have a talent, idea, or a concept, it may be worth developing it and putting it to good use. There are probably more "rags to riches" stories to be found among artists, entertainers, and inventors than among entrepreneurs or employees. Furthermore, you would not have to give up your "day job" to pursue this pathway while obtaining financial independence via the gainful employment and investments pathways. For example, an invention conceived and created on personal time (and not on company time or on company resources) may provide entrepreneurial opportunities to yield tremendous amounts of wealth. In this book, I will discuss intellectual property in further detail and explain how you can make substantial wealth via this pathway. Now that we have discussed the four main pathways to financial independence, let's talk about personal finance.

2

From Debt and Unemployment to Investments and Wealth

Securing Gainful Employment

In Chapter 1, we discussed the four main pathways to financial independence. We discussed the importance of gainful employment, the pros and cons of entrepreneurship, the importance of investments, and the great earning potential of an intellectual property. Regardless of your station in life or where you are financially at this time, this book is intended to provide you with a roadmap to achieving financial independence. With that in mind, the first step is simple.

1. Get a job.

While a high paying job would be preferred, any job would do if you are unemployed. The idea is to have a source of income upon which you can support yourself. Once you have secured a job, it is important to assess whether you are underemployed. If you are underemployed, your next step is:

2. Find a better job.

This "better job" should either pay you more than your current job or at least provide you with better opportunities for personal growth and advancement than your current job. Now that you have a "better job", you should assess whether you are still underemployed or if there is room for personal advancement with education, training, certification, or professional development. If you are still underemployed, repeat step 2 until you find a job which matches your credentials and educational attainment. If you are adequately employed, your next step is:

3. Increase your earning potential through professional development, education, training, or certification.

If you have followed these steps correctly, you should be making more money and working in a meaningful capacity in a job which is consistent with your educational and personal interests. Hopefully, you are on your way to future promotions and advancement and to gainful employment.

Debt Management

What is debt? In simple terms, debt is pure evil. It is insidious. Because of the nature of compounding interest, today's "big" debt can easily become tomorrow's "huge" debt. Debt is not static. It grows and grows exponentially and must be kept in check and eliminated altogether. For this reason, if you have any kind of debt whatsoever, you must act now. The time to act is to today. Not tomorrow. Not next week.

Now that you have secured employment, it is imperative that you assess your debt situation. In general, there is "good" debt and there is "bad" debt. Good debt would include mortgage debt and student loans. Bad debt would include any other line of credit which has an interest rate associated with it. This may include a car loan, credit card debt, a personal loan, and the like. Because of the nature of compounding interest, bad debt should be kept at a minimum and paid off as quickly as possible. For this reason, if you have any bad debt, you will want to determine how much bad debt you have and the interest rate associated with each bad debt account. Once you have paid off all of your bad debt, you will want to pay off your good debt as well. Truth be told, while some debt may offer tax advantages, debt is debt.

As such, having debt, good or bad, is a hindrance to becoming financially independent.

4. Characterize all of your debt.

Let's say you have the following debts: a car loan, credit card debt, mortgage, personal loan, and a student loan. Your first step in managing your debt is to characterize all of your debt. This entails determining the debt amount, the interest rate for each debt type, the minimum payment amount, and the debt characterization – either good or bad. On the following page is a debt characterization table. From this debt characterization table, you can determine how much debt you owe, the minimum amount you need to pay each month towards your debts, and which debts need to be paid off first.

Type of Debt	Debt Amount	Interest Rate	Minimum Payment	Debt Characterization
Car Loan	$3,000	5%	$150	Bad Debt
Credit Card	$500	18%	$10	Bad Debt
Mortgage	$80,000	6%	$600	Good Debt
Personal Loan	$5,000	10%	$100	Bad Debt
Student Loan	$10,000	7%	$200	Good Debt

In this example, your total debt amount is $98,500 (and counting due to the nature of compounding interest). The minimum monthly payment amount that you need to be paying towards your debt is $1,060. It should be noted that you need to be earning more than $1,060 a month to cover your debts and your cost of living. If not, then you need to consider reducing your cost of living by making lifestyle changes and/or finding more gainful employment.

Let's say that you are gainfully employed and that you have $1,200 a month that you can pay towards all of your debt. Your next task is to determine how much bad debt you have and which account among your bad debt has the highest interest rate. In this example, you owe $8,500 in bad debt and the account with the highest interest rate is the credit card. Your next step is:

5. MAKE CONSISTENT *MINIMUM* PAYMENTS TOWARDS *ALL* DEBT WITH *EXTRA* PAYMENTS TOWARDS THE *BAD* DEBT WITH THE *HIGHEST* INTEREST RATE.

In this example, you would make the minimum payment for all of your accounts except for the credit card account since it has the highest interest rate. Excluding the credit card account, that minimum payment amount would be $1,050. For the credit card account, however, you would make a payment of $150 and not $10. By making monthly payments of $1,200 towards your debt ($1,050 + $150), you will be on the fast track to debt elimination. Within a few months, you will have eliminated all credit card debt and will be able to apply this technique to eliminate the debt with the next highest interest rate, the personal loan. By eliminating your debt, you are increasing your ***discretionary income*** which will enable you to save and invest in investment vehicles. By eliminating your debt, you are also increasing your ***net worth*** which is essential to becoming financially independent.

Personal Finance Management

Now that you have a grip on your debt and are making payments towards being debt-free, you need to consider a personal finance management tool. The one that I recommend and use is called Mint® (www.mint.com). This tool or website tracks and syncs your checking accounts, savings accounts, and investments, and even some billing accounts - all into one website. It will help you with budgeting and goal setting and, best of all, the service is free. While there are other personal finance management websites, not all of them are free. If you happen to not like Mint® for whatever reason, an alternative website which I would recommend would be Personal Capital® (www.personalcapital.com). Personal Capital® is also free and provides some of the same basic features as Mint®. Some may prefer Mint® over Personal Capital® while others may prefer Personal Capital® over Mint®. Regardless of your preference, you should be using one of these powerful personal finance management tools to the utmost to get a birds' eye view of your finances and to keep track of your financial progress.

6. Go online and register an account with Mint® or Personal Capital®.

Money Management

At this point, you are ready to see some significant changes to your financial situation. You are paying down your debt and are freeing yourself from financial bondage. You are setting the foundation for good financial habits which will serve you well for a lifetime. You are conquering your debt and are increasing your net worth. You are improving your station in life. While others are spending beyond their means, you are exercising discipline and showing self-restraint. While others are still shackled to debt, you are liberating yourself from its grasps. You are making the transition from having "bad" debt to having only "good" debt. **You are truly pulling yourself up by your bootstraps.**

Once you have eliminated all bad debts, it is time for you to start investing. For some of you, upon being hired, you had the option to enroll in a 401(k). But what is a 401(k) and is it right for you? A 401(k) is a retirement plan that an employer provides for his or her employees. In many such plans, an employee may contribute up to 15% of his or her pre-tax salary every year towards their retirement. Money contributed to a 401(k) grows tax-free and does not get taxed until it is withdrawn. In addition, many 401(k) plans have an employer matching contribution up to a certain percentage. For example, let's say you make $40,000 a year and you enroll in your company's 401(k) plan which has a maximum contribution limit of 15% and an employer matching contribution up to 5%. If you elect to contribute the maximum amount possible towards your retirement, you would be investing $6,000 + $2,000 a year (15% of your money plus 5% of *your employer's money*) towards retirement. That's $2,000 a year of "free" money! In essence, your employer is rewarding you dollar-for-dollar (up to 5%) with free money for investing in your own retirement. This is a great bargain! For this reason, I strongly adjure you to enroll in your company's 401(k) plan.

7. Enroll in your company's 401(k) and contribute *at least* the employer matching contribution amount.

But what if your company does not offer a 401(k)? Not all companies do. If your company does not provide a 401(k), then an IRA account is your next best option. An IRA or individual retirement account is an investment vehicle similar to a 401(k) but is not provided by your employer. Another difference between a 401(k) and an IRA is the maximum contribution limit per year. As of 2018, a 401(k) has a maximum contribution limit of $18,500 per year while an IRA has a maximum contribution limit of $5,500 per year.[8],[9] There are two types of IRAs – traditional IRAs and Roth IRAs. Contributions to a traditional IRA are tax-deductible while contributions to a Roth IRA are not tax-deductible. Withdrawals upon retirement for a traditional IRA are taxed; however, withdrawals and earnings upon retirement for a Roth IRA are tax-free.

So which IRA is right for you? That is another difficult question for me to answer for you. Nonetheless, there are some considerations to

---

[8] Internal Revenue Service, Retirement Topics – 401(k) and Profit-Sharing Plan Contribution Limits, *available at* https://www.irs.gov/retirement-plans/plan-participant-employee/retirement-topics-401k-and-profit-sharing-plan-contribution-limits (*last updated Oct. 24, 2017*).

[9] Internal Revenue Service, Retirement Topics – IRA Contribution Limits, *available at* https://www.irs.gov/retirement-plans/plan-participant-employee/retirement-topics-ira-contribution-limits (*last updated Oct. 20, 2017*).

consider. If you are already in a high tax bracket, then a traditional IRA may be right for you. A traditional IRA would provide you with a yearly tax deduction for your contributions which may translate into more savings in terms of taxes owed every year. If you are currently not in a high tax bracket, then a Roth IRA may be better. Upon retirement, your large nest egg which you have accumulated in your Roth IRA will not be taxed and you will be able to enjoy all of your retirement savings from that account free of taxation.

8. Enroll in a traditional or Roth IRA.

Can you have both a 401(k) and an IRA? Absolutely! In fact, you should. As a general rule, however, you should maximize your contribution to your 401(k) first before contributing to your IRA to take advantage of the 'free money' by way of the employer matching contribution. Only after you have maximized your contributions to your 401(k) and IRA for the year should you consider making non-retirement investments. Before we talk about non-retirement investments, however, you also may be wondering how you should be investing with your 401(k) and/or IRA.

There are many investment strategies when it comes to investing. For the sake of brevity, however, I will say there are two types of approaches. One approach is investing for ***growth***. Investing for growth entails investing in stocks or mutual funds which have great earning potential. Growth stocks and mutual funds are generally more volatile in the short term but offer higher rates of return in the long term. For this reason, growth stocks and mutual funds are ideal for younger investors who have more time on their hands to weather the highs and lows of market swings and for aggressive investors who are looking for greater rates of return.

The other approach is investing for ***income***. This approach entails investing in stocks or mutual funds which are largely consistent in paying dividends. These stocks and mutual funds are generally less volatile but also offer lower rates of return. For this reason, income stocks and mutual funds are ideal for older investors who are closer to retirement and for those conservative investors who have less tolerance for market swings.

If you are still not sure which investment strategy is right for you, then consider keeping it simple and investing in a low-cost index fund which follows the S&P 500. An index fund is a mutual fund which models or mimics the market as a whole. Because the market, over time, is always climbing, you are very likely to earn a good return over the life of your investment. Also, because an index fund includes a large number of stocks, the fund is well diversified and the risk of investment is greatly reduced.

9. Invest in a growth, income, or index mutual fund via your 401(k) and/or IRA.

Now that you have invested in your 401(k) and/or your IRA, you need to evaluate your living expenses and your financial goals in life. If you are currently paying a mortgage but cannot deduct the mortgage interests from your taxes, then you should consider paying off this debt as soon as possible. While mortgage debt is generally considered to be a good debt, it is not a good debt if there is no tax benefit. Furthermore, because of the nature of compounding interest, you will be paying far more for your home than the sticker price if you do not make additional principal payments towards paying off your mortgage. Keep in mind, however, that every dollar spent on additional principal payments is a dollar not spent towards investments. Depending on your mortgage interest rates, however, it very well may make more sense to pay off your mortgage.

10. IF YOU CANNOT DEDUCT YOUR MORTGAGE INTEREST FROM YOUR TAXES, CONSIDER MAKING ADDITIONAL PRINCIPAL PAYMENTS TOWARDS YOUR MORTGAGE TO PAY IT OFF.

If you are currently renting, then consider buying a home. Homeownership is part of the American dream. Homeownership is also an accomplishment but it is not for everyone. These are just a few of the questions to consider when thinking about buying a home:

For how long do you plan on living in the area?

Will you need to make a sizeable down payment?

Are you currently paying too much for rent?

Do you have reasonably good credit?

For many people, it is easier to qualify for an apartment than it is to qualify for a mortgage. Nonetheless, it is generally much cheaper to pay a mortgage than it is to pay rent. While this may provide you with some financial incentive to buy a home, there are some other considerations as well. The down payment needed to buy a home can be sizeable, usually up to 20% of the value of the home. Once you purchase your home, when something breaks or needs maintenance, you will have to fix it or do it yourself. Despite these inconvenient truths, the benefits of homeownership generally outweigh those of renting if you can afford the down payment and plan on living in the area for a least a few years.

11. IF YOU ARE RENTING, CONSIDER BUYING A HOME.

At this point, you may be wondering how you are going to save enough money to make a down payment on a home. If you do not have one already, you will need a savings account and/or a money-market account. Savings accounts offer lower rates of interest and have no check writing features. Money market accounts, on the other hand, offer higher rates of interest than savings accounts and limited check writing features. Money market accounts also require a larger minimum balance amount. The type of account that you may wish to open is entirely up to you but an interest-bearing money market account would be advisable. Since you are looking to accumulate and save a considerable amount of money in this account, it would make sense to utilize the principle of compounding interest to have your money earn money for you while striving to save as much money as possible.

12. OPEN A SAVINGS ACCOUNT AND/OR A MONEY MARKET ACCOUNT.

Now that you have opened a savings and/or money market account, it is time to set some savings goals. The first goal should be to save enough money for a family emergency. Life happens and you should always have at least enough money to purchase a plane ticket to visit a family member in a time of need. The second goal should be to save enough money for a "rainy day". By "rainy day", I mean *unemployment, illness or injury*. If for whatever reason, you should lose your job or find yourself unemployed, you need to be able to support yourself financially for at least six months. For example, if you currently make $2,000 a month, you should save at least $12,000 for a rainy day in the event that you should lose your job. Your third goal should be to save enough money for a down payment towards a home. This amount will depend largely on the amount of home you wish to buy, but more exactly, it will depend on the amount of home that you can afford.

13. SET SAVINGS GOALS FOR YOURSELF.

To determine the amount of home you can afford, you will want to use a mortgage calculator. A mortgage calculator will tell you how much your monthly payment will be for a given home price (loan amount), down payment, interest rate, and mortgage term. A good mortgage calculator will also tell you how much interest you will pay over the life of the loan. There are many mortgage calculators available for personal use on the internet. Once you have found a mortgage calculator, you can play with the numbers to get a feel for how each parameter affects your monthly payment. A good mortgage calculator which I would recommend can be found at www.bankrate.com. Once you are at the Bankrate® website, type in a search for "mortgage calculator". A list of options will appear. Choose the option which is right for you and your situation. A good place to start would be

https://www.bankrate.com/calculators/mortgages/mortgage-calculator.aspx.

This calculator works best for those who are interested in fixed mortgages as opposed to adjustable rate mortgages or ARM. If you think an ARM loan would be best for you, then type in a search for "ARM calculator" or go to

https://www.bankrate.com/calculators/mortgages/adjustable-rate-mortgage-arm-calculator.aspx.

Either way, it would behoove you to get a feel for how much homeownership would cost you in the short and long run and how terms such as interest rates and mortgage term can affect home affordability.

14. Use a Mortgage Calculator to Determine How Much Home You Can Afford.

At this point, you may be thinking to yourself that saving money is fine and dandy but how am I going to save that much money when I have bills to pay? The answer is simple. ***Pay yourself first through automatic savings***. In addition to evaluating each and every bill or expense you have, you need to pay yourself first. The easiest way to pay yourself first is to set up your checking account to automatically transfer funds over to your savings and/or money market account. Another way to pay yourself first is to request that a portion of your paycheck be direct deposited into your savings and/or money market account. If you are able to save $25 a week into an interest-bearing savings account, at the end of the year, you will have at least $1,300 in savings. What if you double that amount and save $50 a week? Saving $50 a week would give you at least $2,600 in savings at the end of the year. What if you double that amount and save $100 a week? Saving $100 a week would give you at least $5,200 in savings at the end of the year. And what if you even double that amount? Saving $200 a week would give you at least $10,400 in savings at the end of the year. Hopefully, as you can see, the more you are willing to save, the sooner you will accumulate substantial savings towards that house you wish to buy or even some other financial goal or asset you wish to acquire.

15. Pay yourself first through automatic savings.

As an aside to automatic savings, there are also micro-investing options you may wish to consider as well. Micro-investing expands on the concept of automatic savings. With micro-investing, you can direct your weekly savings to be invested in a number of different investments with varying investing strategies. There are, however, a few caveats. These services are generally not free and there is no guaranteed interest rate at which your investments will grow. Like any other securities investment, there will be ups and downs but a mostly net positive return on investment over the long run. Depending on how long you may wish to save or invest, this option may be right for you. Two popular websites for micro-investing are STASH® (www.stashinvest.com) and Acorns (www.acorns.com). It should also be noted that, at the time of this writing, Acorns offers its services for free to college students who sign up with a valid .edu email address.

16. CONSIDER PAYING YOURSELF FIRST THROUGH MICRO-INVESTING.

If you have implemented all sixteen of these steps, then you are well on your way to creating some serious wealth and achieving financial independence. At this point, you may be wondering why I did not suggest buying a house as an investment vehicle. The reason is quite simple. *A house is a place to live, not an investment.* By merely having a house, you are not making money. While it is true that you are saving money by not renting, the primary purpose of a house is to provide a roof over your head, not to "get rich quick". This is not to say, however, that money cannot be made in real estate. It can be. But the nature of making money in real estate is that it requires a lot of capital which may be beyond the scope of practicality for most people. Real estate investing can also be notoriously risky and may not be worth risking all that you have worked so hard for.

If you absolutely feel that you must invest in real estate, then consider investing in a REIT instead. A REIT or real estate investment trust is a company which owns and operates income-producing real estate.[10] From an investor point-of-view, a REIT is like a mutual fund

---

10 Nareit, "What's a REIT?", available at https://www.reit.com/what-reit (last visited on July 5, 2018).

comprising a diverse array of income-producing real estate properties. By law, a REIT must pay out at least 90% of its taxable income to its shareholders as dividends.[11] For this reason, REITs make great investment vehicles. If you wish to make money in real estate without the trouble, headache, and risk that is often associated with real estate investing, then a REIT would be the way to go.

17. CONSIDER INVESTING IN A REIT.

---

11 *Id.*

3

LIFESTYLE CONSIDERATIONS

Now that I have provided you with a roadmap to wealth through gainful employment and investments, let's talk about lifestyle. Being financially independent is a lifestyle choice. The equation is simple. If you decide to spend more than you earn, you will not become financially independent. Furthermore, if you are currently financially independent and you choose to spend more than you earn, you will not be financially independent for very long. For this reason, you need to consider your lifestyle wisely and live within your means. This is one of the reasons why I recommend a personal finance management tool such as Mint® or Personal Capital® as an essential step towards financial independence. With either one of these tools, you instantly get a better feel for how you spend your money and where you can improve. The ability to make necessary lifestyle changes, however, will be crucial to your success in becoming financially independent and maintaining your financial independence status.

Lifestyle Changes

What is a lifestyle change? A lifestyle change is a change in habits which will have a positive and direct impact on your ability to become and remain financially independent. For example, one of the barriers to becoming financially independent is buying more house and more car than you can afford. A house and a car are big ticket items which often sink the dreams of many people who wish to become financially independent because they carry a hefty price tag as well as incur interest over time. In many ways, these items are essential but will you ever really need a five-bedroom house with an indoor swimming pool? Probably not. You can save yourself a considerable amount of money if you are willing to buy a home which meets your present and current needs. Likewise, if you are willing to pay full price for a used, reliable vehicle in lieu of financing a brand new luxury car, then you will be saving yourself thousands of dollars. Not only will you be saving a considerable amount of money, you will also be better able to invest in yourself and increase your earning potential.

At the following website, you will find an article written by Kathleen Elkins of Business Insider promoting some lifestyle changes which I highly endorse.

http://www.businessinsider.com/lifestyle-changes-to-save-more-money-2015-11

This article lists twenty-one lifestyle changes which are sure to put more money in your pocket and to clear your pathway to financial independence. Some of these lifestyle changes include cutting cable television.[12] Cable is one of many services for which many Americans pay too much. The average cable bill in the United States is about $100 a month.[13] That translates into $1,200 a year for just a handful of useful channels and a bunch of useless channels for which most people could care less. By cutting the cable, you could be saving yourself literally thousands of dollars and improving your net worth.

Does cutting the cable mean that you are doomed to a life of boredom and lackluster entertainment? Not at all. Ideally speaking, instead of

---

[12] Elkins, Kathleen (2015). *"21 Lifestyle Changes to Make If You Want to Save Money."*, available at http://www.businessinsider.com/lifestyle-changes-to-save-more-money-2015-11 (*last visited on July 5, 2018*).

[13] Breen, Marcia (2015). *"Cable and Satellite TV Costs Will Climb Again in 2016."*, available at https://www.nbcnews.com/business/business-news/cable-satellite-tv-costs-will-climb-again-2016-n484531 (*last visited on July 5, 2018*)

watching television, you could spend more time investing in yourself by reading, exercising, or learning a new skill. If you absolutely must have televised entertainment, however, I would recommend a good internet connection and streaming services such as Netflix, Hulu, or Sling TV®. For about $8 a month, you can enjoy some high-quality content on Netflix or Hulu. For $25 a month, you can enjoy many of your favorite cable channels on Sling TV®. These services are very reliable and are sure to provide you with great content at a low price compared to cable or satellite TV.

What are some other lifestyle changes that you should consider? Here are the twenty-one lifestyle changes suggested by Kathleen Elkins.[14] I highly recommend that you read her article.

1. Record all of the money you spend. (Mint® does this for you.)

2. Go homemade. (Eat at home instead of eating out.)

3. Grocery shop on a full stomach.

4. Make bigger and fewer trips to the grocery store.

5. Withdraw money exclusively from your bank's ATM.

---

14 Elkins, Kathleen (2015). *"21 Lifestyle Changes to Make If You Want to Save Money.", available at* http://www.businessinsider.com/lifestyle-changes-to-save-more-money-2015-11 *(last visited July 5, 2018).*

6. Stop buying a daily coffee.

7. Automate your finances.

8. Go cash-only.

9. Cancel your underused subscriptions and start paying 'a la carte'.

10. Have the hard money talks with your spouse.

11. Ditch name-brand products. (Buy generic whenever possible.)

12. Cut cable.

13. Buy less meat.

14. Create a no-spend day. (This is a day of the week on which you do not spend any money.)

15. Buy food seasonally.

16. Pay more than the minimum balance on your credit cards.

17. Stop buying fast food.

18. Start hanging out with people you admire.

19. Unplug your electronics when you aren't using them.

20. Get used to spending money now that will save you money later. (Invest in things that will save you money.)

21. Take pleasure in living simply and using less.

By incorporating these and other lifestyle changes, you will save yourself some money and will have more money to pay down debt and to invest.

Financial Goals

In addition to making lifestyle changes, it is crucial to set financial goals. Without financial goals, you can easily lose focus as to why you are trying to save in the first place. With reasonable financial goals, you can more purposefully save and achieve them. There are many financial goals that you can set for yourself. Reasonable financial goals which everyone should have are:

1. Saving for a rainy day.

2. Getting out of debt.

3. Saving for retirement.

In fact, these goals are paramount to becoming financially independent. Other financial goals may include saving for college or saving for a home. With a personal finance management website such as Mint®, not only can you name your financial goals on the website, you can even attach savings and investment accounts to them as well.

Hopefully, now that you have written down or logged your financial goals into Mint®, you need to make your goals more tangible. To make your goals more tangible, you will want to provide dollar amounts for each of these goals. For example, let's start with saving for a rainy day. The amount you save for a rainy day will be unique to you and will differ from that of your neighbor or anyone else. If you make $2,000 a month, you should write down or log into your Mint® account "$12,000" as your savings goals for saving for a rainy day. By writing down or logging $12,000 as your savings goal for a rainy day, you have taken an intangible goal (save money for a rainy day) and made it tangible (save $12,000 for a rainy day). Similarly, for your goal of getting out of debt, you will want to determine how much total debt you have and record that dollar amount or log it into your Mint® account. Likewise, for your goal of saving for retirement, you will want to determine how much money you will need to retire comfortably at the age in which you want to retire. For example, if you want to retire at age 50, you will need to have saved more money than if you wish to retire at age 65. You will need to determine how much income you will need to live comfortably in your retirement years.

As a side note, it should be stated that retirement may not be for everyone. Many people who retire often find themselves working part-time or in some capacity, not out of financial need but out of boredom. For this reason, it is imperative that you find a vocation that you enjoy and make retirement an optional goal for yourself. By doing a job that you truly love, you are doing yourself a huge favor and your mental health with thank you for it. Regardless of whether you wish to retire, you should take advantage of the tax benefits of investing for retirement. Not only will your investments grow faster, but you will also be rewarding yourself with a nice nest egg in your golden years. Furthermore, you will also be preparing yourself in the event that you are forced into early retirement due to sickness or injury.

4

INCOME FOR LIFE THROUGH INTELLECTUAL PROPERTY

Now that we have discussed making money through gainful employment and financial investments, let's change gears and talk about making money through intellectual property. Merriam-Webster defines "intellectual property" as "property (such as an idea, invention, or process) that derives from the work of the mind or intellect".[15] While intellectual property covers many things, in a practical sense and for the purposes of this book, an intellectual property is a copyright, a patent, or a trademark. All three of these types of intellectual property have legal protections and are designed to promote creativity and ingenuity for the benefit of society as a whole.

---

15 Merriam-Webster Dictionary, *available at* https://www.merriam-webster.com (last updated July 2, 2018).

COPYRIGHTS

A copyright is a legal protection which prevents others from copying, selling, or producing derivative work from your copyrightable work. A key requirement of a copyrightable work is that the work must be "fixed in a tangible medium of expression".[16] For most people, books come to mind as a copyrightable work, however, copyrights are not limited just to books. There are eight categories of copyrightable works.[17] Those categories are[18]:

1. Literary, musical and dramatic works.

2. Pantomimes and choreographic works.

3. Pictorial, graphic and sculptural works.

4. Sound recordings.

5. Motion pictures and other audiovisual works.

6. Computer programs.

7. Compilations of works and derivative works.

8. Architectural works.

---

16 Purdue University, University Copyright Office, *Copyright Basics – Copyright Overview*, https://www.lib.purdue.edu/uco/CopyrightBasics/basics.html (*last visited July 6, 2018*).
17 *Id.*
18 *Id.*

One of the benefits of copyright is that your work is protected as soon as it is in a tangible medium. For example, if you decide to write a book or create a computer program, you are instantly afforded copyright protection for your work without any additional steps on your part. While this is absolutely true, many people take the additional step of registering their copyrighted work. Registration of a copyrighted work with the US government is necessary in order to bring an infringement lawsuit to court in the United States. A copyrightable work may be registered online with the federal government at www.copyright.gov for $35.[19] Alternatively, a paper application for registration of a copyright with the federal government has an $85 fee.[20]

Patents

The US Patent and Trademark Office defines a patent as "a limited duration property right relating to an invention, granted by the United States Patent and Trademark Office in exchange for public disclosure of the invention".[21] In particular, a patent is a right to

---

[19] U.S. Copyright Office, *Circular 4*, available at https://www.copyright.gov/circs/circ04.pdf (*last visited on July 7, 2018*).
[20] *Id.*
[21] U.S. Patent and Trademark Office, *Patent FAQs*, https://www.uspto.gov/help/patent-help (*last modified on Dec. 5, 2016*).

exclude others from making, using, selling or otherwise profiting from your invention.[22] For example, let's say that you invent a great device or machine which can make life much easier for all of humanity. In a society without patent rights, someone could copy your invention, sell it, and compete against you with your very own inventive design without making any intellectual effort whatsoever. Not only is this not fair to you as the inventor, it hurts society as a whole because true inventors such as yourself would be very reluctant to disclose their inventions if their genius could be so easily exploited. For this reason, inventors are afforded patent rights to exclude others from using their inventions for a limited amount of time (twenty years in the US) so that they may fully benefit from the manufacture and sale of their inventions.

TRADEMARKS

According to the US Patent and Trademark Office, a trademark is "a word, phrase, symbol, and/or design that identifies and distinguishes the source of the goods of one party from those of others".[23] Trademarks are one of the hallmarks of consumerism. There

---

22 35 U.S.C. §154(a)(1)
23 U.S. Patent and Trademark Office, *Trademark, Patent, or Copyright?*, available at https://www.uspto.gov/trademarks-getting-started/trademark-basics/trademark-patent-or-copyright (*last modified on June 9, 2016*).

are many famous brands out there and each brand is known for its quality of goods and services. One of the benefits of a trademark is that it sets you as well as your goods and services apart from others. For example, let's say that you decide to go into the ice cream making business. To set yourself apart from Breyers® Ice Cream and a flavorless, generic, store brand ice cream, you need a trademark. You need some sort of logo or design which says "I represent quality."

The power of trademarks can be very profound. Many goods that we use today are referred to by their trademark names. For example, some may unconsciously request a Kleenex® instead of asking for a tissue. Others may request a glass of Kool-Aid® instead of a glass of flavored water. Hopefully, as you can see, the more pervasive the trademark name, the more effective the marketing is.

Making Money through Intellectual Property

There are many benefits to making money through intellectual property. One of the benefits is that making money through intellectual property can be personally rewarding. For example, writing a book or a movie script can be an arduous task. Nonetheless, once you have finished writing a book or a script, you can hold your head up high and say "I wrote that." It is an accomplishment in and of itself which can be very rewarding.

In addition to the sense of accomplishment, however, there is the prospect of making money. A book can be published and sold in bookstores nationwide. A movie script could be read by the right movie director and bought for "the right price". Not only would you make money for selling the script, but you would have the honor of seeing your movie on the big screen. Depending on your personal goals or even your calling in life, creating intellectual property may be your ticket to unlimited streams of revenue.

One of the exciting things about making money through an intellectual property is that you are putting your creative energy to work. This could be a leisurely pursuit or a lifelong hobby. It could even become your new vocation as an inventor, songwriter, or photographer. Whatever the case may be, intellectual property allows you to utilize your talents and promote yourself to the world. One of the basic premises of the book <u>Think and Grow Rich</u> by Napoleon Hill is the use of the intellect to find that niche in society which you can fill. By putting your mind to work, you are creating opportunities for yourself which can be very rewarding and become a source of income for life.

WORDS OF ADVICE ON COPYRIGHTS, PATENTS, AND TRADEMARKS

Now that we have discussed copyrights, patents, and trademarks as well as making money through intellectual property, here is some practical advice. With regards to copyrights, copyright protections are afforded to anyone who produces a copyrightable work which is "fixed in a tangible medium of expression". However, if you want to bring a lawsuit against someone for copyright infringement, you need to have had your work registered with the federal government. Registration of a copyright is a totally voluntary process. Nonetheless, it is highly recommended for most works. A possible exception would be photographs. Photographs are copyrightable works. A photographer, however, may have many hundreds if not thousands of images on hand. Because of the sheer number of images that a photographer may have, it would probably be impractical and not advisable to pay $35 for the online registration of each photograph. A few photographs may be warranted but most likely, not all.

With regards to patents, my strongest advice would be to hire a patent attorney or a patent agent to prosecute an application for patent on your behalf before the US Patent and Trademark Office. Patent applications are routinely rejected by patent examiners because of the broad nature of their claims. I know this for a fact because I used to be a patent examiner. A good patent attorney or a patent agent can skillfully craft claim language for your patent application to overcome rejection and to get it approved.

You might be wondering what the difference between a patent attorney and a patent agent is. A patent attorney is a person who graduated from law school, passed the patent bar exam, and is registered to prosecute patent applications before the US Patent and Trademark Office. A patent agent, however, is a non-law school graduate who has passed the patent bar exam and is registered to prosecute patent applications before the US Patent and Trademark Office. While both patent attorneys and patent agents can represent inventors before the US Patent and Trademark Office, only patent attorneys can represent inventors in US courts for patent infringement cases.

With regards to trademarks, trademarks are mostly the domain of the entrepreneur. While one may wish to design his or her own trademark logo for their business, another alternative is to buy an existing trademark from a trademark owner. This route is faster than the route of applying for a trademark and hoping that your trademark application gets approved. Regardless of which route you take, I would strongly advise you to hire the services of a trademark attorney. A trademark attorney can perform comprehensive searches to help streamline and facilitate the process of securing a trademark on your behalf.

5

ADDITIONAL TOOLS TO CONSIDER

BUILDING YOUR CREDIT

Having good credit is important and is an indication of good financial health. If you have a tremendous amount of debt, however, chances are, you also have a poor credit rating. While not the focus of this book, it should be noted that having a good credit rating is important for obtaining a favorable interest rate on a mortgage or any other line of credit. Generally speaking, I would advise ***against*** applying for credit unless it is a mortgage or a student loan. Nonetheless, in limited instances, it may make sense to have a credit card for making hotel and airline reservations or to build credit. If you feel that you must have a credit card, you should observe certain rules.

1. Never borrow more than you can pay back in full.

2. Pay off the balance in full each month.

3. Never miss a payment.

One of the tools that I recommend for monitoring credit is a website called Credit Karma (www.creditkarma.com). This free website provides current, up-to-date information regarding your credit score and access to your Equifax and Transunion credit reports. By monitoring your credit with Credit Karma, you can stay in touch with your credit information and improve your overall financial health. You will also have the peace of mind of knowing exactly where you stand financially in case you ever need to borrow a loan from a lender.

Self-Directed Brokerage Accounts

One of the purposes of a self-directed brokerage account is to provide access to the stock market which has historically only been available through a stockbroker. By circumventing the stockbroker, you are saving yourself the cost of his or her commission by having direct access to the stock market. While investment decisions are entirely up to you with a self-directed brokerage account, you do not have to be ill-informed. Self-brokerage accounts such as TD Ameritrade® (www.tdameritrade.com) and E*TRADE® (www.etrade.com) have an abundant amount of financial and investing information for those who are willing to take the time to learn and to benefit from the vast amount of educational resources that these brokerages have to offer. These brokerages also provide free customer support for those who need assistance with navigating their websites. A self-directed brokerage account is also great for those who know exactly what they would like to invest in. For example, if you know that you wish to invest in an index fund which follows the S&P 500, with TD Ameritrade® or E*TRADE®, you can easily search for index funds using a mutual fund screener and determine which fund has the lowest operating costs and start investing.

529 Plans

If you have children and wish to invest in their educational future, one tax-advantaged investment vehicle to consider is a 529 plan. A 529 plan is an educational savings plan which allows you to save for educational expenses for yourself, your children, or grandchildren.[24] There are, however, restrictions to keep in mind. As an educational savings plan, withdrawal is limited only to qualified education expenses. Withdrawals for qualified education expenses are tax-free. If withdrawals are made for nonqualified expenses, you must pay taxes on that amount as well as a 10% penalty fee.[25]

---

24 U.S. Securities and Exchange Commission, *Introduction to 529 Plans*, available at https://www.sec.gov/reportspubs/investor-publications/investorpubsintro529htm.html (*last modified on May 29, 2018*).

25 *Id.*

Conclusion

There are many pathways to great financial wealth. But there are many roadblocks and obstacles as well. If you have debt, you need to act now to get rid of it. If you are living beyond your means, you need to consider making some lifestyle changes. If you are underemployed, you need to find a new line of work as soon as possible. Your goal of financial independence is achievable and is within your power to achieve. With the steps and advice offered in this book, you are well-equipped to pull yourself up by your bootstraps and start earning and making money. Financial independence is within your reach. Good luck.

About The Author

Michael Fleming is a professionally licensed environmental engineer and a former patent examiner with the US Patent and Trademark Office. He is also author of the book <u>Bootstraps: A Step-by-Step Guide from Debt to Financial Independence</u>.

www.ingramcontent.com/pod-product-compliance
Lightning Source LLC
Chambersburg PA
CBHW052118070526
44584CB00017B/2538